THE MASTER'S *Touch*

Overcoming Depression

By Joseph Barbour and Donna Steiner
Psychological Consultant: Dr. Buddy Mendez

CPH.
SAINT LOUIS

Edited by Roger Sonnenberg and Thomas J. Doyle

1 2 3 4 5 6 7 8 9 10   05 04 03 02 01 00 99 98 97 96

Contents

1. Depression: What Is It?   5
2. Depression: What's the Reason?   15
3. Depression:
   How Can I Cope with It?   26
4. Depression:
   How Can I Help Others?   39

Leaders Notes

Session 1   50
Session 2   54
Session 3   58
Session 4   62

Depression: What Is It?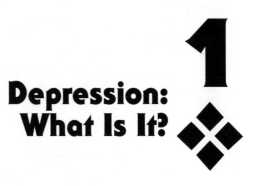

Focusing Our Sights

Depression is on the rise. Studies show that people born in the last 25 years are three to four times more likely to be depressed than those born in previous generations. In this first session we'll define depression by studying its symptoms. We'll also study God's Word for hope and help in dealing with depression.

Focusing Our Attention

Experts tell us that the majority of people experience depression at one time or another. For some it is short-lived. For others it may be as it was for Winston Churchill who said depression followed him around like a "black dog." Despite the fact that so many people seem to talk about depression, and even experience it at times, there are many misunderstandings about it.

1. Check your knowledge of depression by indicating which statements you think are true or false.

____ a. Depression is an equal opportunity employer.

____ b. Depression can occur at any age, including infancy.

5

___ c. Genuine Christians do not experience depression.

___ d. Attractive people are less likely to experience depression.

___ e. One effective way to help someone who is depressed is to tell him he's not really depressed after he tells you he is.

___ f. Depression often feeds on itself, breeding more depression.

___ g. Depression can occur because of anger which is turned inward.

___ h. Severe depression can run in families.

___ i. The best way to treat depression is with antidepressant drugs.

___ j. A depressed person who always talks about suicide will more than likely never harm himself.

2. Complete the following sentences:

a. Whenever I consider depression, I think of ...

b. If someone asked me to define depression, I'd say "Depression is ...

Focusing on the Issue

Depression? One expert correctly called it "the common cold of psychopathology." In one way or another, everyone has, is, or will be affected by depression. Though Scripture tells us to "carry each other's burdens," it is difficult to do so if we ourselves don't know about depression, its symptoms, causes, and treatments. In the next four sessions, we will attempt to answer the following questions about depression:

1) Depression: What is it?
2) Depression: What's the reason?
3) Depression: How can I cope with it?
4) Depression: How can I help others?

As we answer the question "What is depression?" we will discover two things:

- There are certain telltale symptoms of depression.
- Depression is no respecter of persons.

1. Listed below are some actual case studies of people who experienced depression. With pen in hand underline the symptom(s) each person seemed to experience as he/she faced depression. (Note that you are to underline the symptoms, not the causes of depression. You will do that in session 2.)

a. JoAnne has experienced depression for years. As she was growing up, JoAnne was passed from one foster home to another. Her biological mother had tried to care for her when she was 10 but was unable to because of a continuing drug problem. Though JoAnne finished high school, she often went through periods of serious depression. Recently her depression has worsened. She is now unable to go to work. She wants only to sleep. Sometimes she sleeps up to 18 hours a day.

7

❖

b. Though his father died several months ago, Larry has had difficulty coping with life without him. For years Larry and his father ran the family business in partnership. Despite the fact that Larry was being groomed to take over the business upon his father's retirement, he depended on his father immensely. Since his father's death, Larry has lost almost 25 pounds.

c. Elaine left her mother's bedside to run some errands. While gone, her mother died. She has not been able to forgive herself. She tells her best friend, "I'll feel guilty the rest of my life for what I did."

d. John and Mary have been married for two years. They are both in their twenties. Though their sexual relationship had been good, it suddenly decreased to almost nothing after John lost his job unexpectedly. Though he sends resumes, he's been unable to get another job. He spends most of his time in front of the television set.

e. Everyone said Eleda was one of the best choir directors the church ever had; however, recently she seems to have lost interest. "She was always so excited and enthusiastic about what she did," one of the choir members said, "but now she doesn't seem to acquire any pleasure at all out of directing. She seems almost too tired to even lift her arms." Her recent physical exam showed that she had low blood sugar.

f. Darlene's husband has just left her and her three children for another woman. She has never worked outside the home. He gives her very little financial support and the small amount she receives from the state makes her *wonder if she can even go on with life. At times, she even contemplates suicide.*

g. Early in their marriage, Carlos' wife had an affair with his brother. Though he and his wife were separated for a while, they eventually reconciled. However, Carlos never felt that he had dealt adequately with his anger toward his wife and his brother. He is afraid to tell his wife how he feels in fear that she will go back to his brother or into the arms of someone else. He finds himself often getting depressed. Though he has a good job, he's convinced it won't last. Though he has good children, he fears they'll rebel and hang out with the wrong crowd. Everything looks bleak.

h. Chuck is an engineer. He was always considered one of the best in his company; however, his upcoming retirement is worrying him. He is often found staring at his computer. When his colleagues speak to him, he frequently seems to be in another world.

Besides those symptoms mentioned in the case studies, other symptoms can be evident in someone who is depressed. Such symptoms might include a deterioration of one's hygiene and personal care, isolation, being overly concerned about the smallest details, shame, and a feeling of worthlessness.

2. Which symptoms have you seen in someone you've known who has experienced depression?

❖

3. Why do you think in the last few years depression is on the rise?

4. Why do you think studies have shown there is little difference between "religious" and "nonreligious" people in terms of depression?

Focusing on God's Word

There was a time when everything was perfect. There was no guilt, no loneliness, no excessive fatigue. However, with sin everything changed.

1. Read the words spoken by people in the Bible. With pen in hand underline the symptoms of depression described by each.

Job said, "For sighing comes to me instead of food; my groans pour out like water. What I feared has come upon me; what I dreaded has happened to me. I have no peace, no quietness; I have no rest, but only turmoil" (Job 3:24–26).

Jonah said, "Now, O LORD, take away my

life, for it is better for me to die than to live" (Jonah 4:3).

Elijah came to a broom tree, sat down under it and prayed that he might die. "I have had enough, LORD," he said. "Take my life; I am no better than my ancestors." Then he lay down under the tree and fell asleep. All at once an angel touched him and said, "Get up and eat." He looked around, and there by his head was a cake of bread baked over hot coals, and a jar of water. He ate and drank and then lay down again" (1 Kings 19:4–6).

Holy Scripture reminds us that with God's help these Old Testament people were able to get through their depression and once again resume the work God had placed before them. The writer of Hebrews reminds us that Jesus understands our "weaknesses," because He was "tempted in every way, just as we are—yet was without sin" (Hebrews 4:15).

In the Garden of Gethsemane, Jesus agonized over the load of sin which He was about to bear on the cross. Underline those words and/or phrases that indicate Jesus' struggle.

❖❖❖❖❖❖❖❖❖❖❖❖❖❖❖❖❖❖❖❖❖❖❖❖❖❖❖

He began to show grief and distress of mind and was deeply depressed. Then He said to them, "My soul is very sad and deeply grieved, so that I am almost dying of sorrow." (Matthew 26:37–38—Amplified Bible)

The Amplified New Testament. Copyright © 1965 The Lockman Foundation. Used by permission.

❖❖❖❖❖❖❖❖❖❖❖❖❖❖❖❖❖❖❖❖❖❖❖❖❖❖❖

When Jesus suffered and died on the cross for the sins of all people, He rescued us from Satan and sin. Nothing can separate us from God's love for us, including the bondage of

❖

depression. Through faith strengthened by the Holy Spirit working through God's Word, He sets us free to live new lives.

2. Read aloud Paul's proclamation.

Therefore, if anyone is in Christ, he is a new creation; the old has gone, the new has come! (2 Corinthians 5:17).

How does this proclamation speak to us who experience depression? who live with those who struggle with depression?

3. Respond to the following statement: "Depression does not have to have the final word! Christ does!"

Focusing on My Life

1. Review the following statements made by some who suffered from depression. Have you or someone you've known made similar statements?

"Depression follows me like a black dog." — Winston Churchill

"If what I feel were equally distributed to the whole human family, there would not be one cheerful face on the earth." — Abraham Lincoln

"There are days I feel so depressed that I feel like I'm walking through the valley of the shadow of death." — a pastor

"I feel like if I only had more faith I wouldn't feel so depressed."—an elder of the church.

2. Someone once said, "If you fail to plan, you plan to fail." Another person said, "Pray to God, but keep rowing to shore." Review the following suggestions for overcoming depression. Which ones have you implemented in your life or suggested to someone you know who's experiencing depression?

- Read the Bible
- Attend worship
- Receive the Lord's Supper
- Counsel with your pastor
- Concentrate on being less introspective
- Help others
- Develop new interests
- Pray
- Other _____
- Other _____

3. Write Psalm 23 on a Post-It note or index card. Place it somewhere in your house or office where you'll see it often.

Focusing on the Week Ahead

Keep a daily journal. Instead of recording

your emotional lows, record your emotional highs! Be sure to describe your feelings during these times.

Closing

As someone reads Psalm 23 slowly, close your eyes. After the reading, spend a few minutes in silent prayer, talking to God about how you're feeling and rejoicing in His promises.

❖

Depression: What's the Reason?

Focusing Our Sights

Just as there are different types of depression and many different symptoms associated with it, so there are many possible causes of depression. In this session we will discuss some of the more common causes. Despite the many reasons for depression, we will rejoice in knowing that through Jesus Christ there is hope.

Focusing Our Attention

Plutarch once wrote: "If you live with a lame man, you will learn to limp."

1. Is depression contagious?

2. If depression isn't contagious, why is it that so many spouses or children of depressed people become distraught and depressed?

3. Describe what it is like to live or to work with someone who is/was always depressed?

4. We have been taught from Scripture: "As a man thinketh, so he becometh." If all you ever hear from a friend is negative thoughts, how might your own thinking or feelings be challenged?

Focusing on the Issue

In our last session we looked at some of the symptoms of depression. Just as there are different symptoms of depression, so there are different causes.

1. Listed below are the same case studies which you looked at last week. This week, with pen in hand underline the cause for each person's depression.

a. JoAnne has experienced depression for years. As she was growing up, JoAnne was passed from one foster home to another. Her biological mother had tried to care for her when she was 10 but was unable to because of a continuing drug problem. Though JoAnne finished high school, she often went through periods of serious depression. Recently her depression has worsened. She is now unable to go to work. She wants only to sleep. Sometimes she sleeps up to 18 hours a day.

b. Though his father died several months ago, Larry has had difficulty coping with life without him. For years Larry and his father ran the family business in partnership. Despite the fact that Larry was being groomed to take over the business upon his father's retirement, he depended on his father immensely. Since his father's death, Larry has lost almost 25 pounds.

c. Elaine left her mother's bedside to run some errands. While gone, her mother died. She has not been able to forgive herself. She tells her best friend, "I'll feel guilty the rest of my life for what I did."

d. John and Mary have been married for two years. They are both in their twenties. Though their sexual relationship had been good, it suddenly decreased to almost nothing after John lost his job unexpectedly. Though he sends resumes, he's been unable to get another job. He spends most of his time in front of the television set.

e. Everyone said Eleda was one of the best choir directors the church ever had; however, recently she seems to have lost interest. "She was always so excited and enthusiastic about what she did," one of the choir members said, "but now she doesn't seem to acquire any pleasure at all out of directing. She seems almost too tired to even lift her arms." Her recent physical exam showed that she had low blood sugar.

f. Darlene's husband has just left her and her three children for another woman. She has never worked outside the home. He gives her very little financial support and the small amount she receives from the state makes her wonder if she can even go on with life. At times, she even contemplates suicide.

g. Early in their marriage, Carlos' wife had

❖

an affair with his brother. Though he and his wife were separated for a while, they eventually reconciled. However, Carlos never felt that he had dealt adequately with his anger toward his wife and his brother. He is afraid to tell his wife how he feels in fear that she will go back to his brother or into the arms of someone else. He finds himself often getting depressed. Though he has a good job, he's convinced it won't last. Though he has good children, he fears they'll rebel and hang out with the wrong crowd. Everything looks bleak.

h. Chuck is an engineer. He was always considered one of the best in his company; however, his upcoming retirement is worrying him. He is often found staring at his computer. When his colleagues speak to him, he frequently seems to be in another world.

Names in Case Studies	Causes of Depression
_____a. JoAnne	1. Physical (e.g., low blood sugar, brain tumor)
_____b. Larry	2. Genetic (e.g., several people across several generations suffer from depression)
_____c. Elaine	3. Triggering Situations (e.g., death, loss of job)
_____d. John	4. Distorted Thinking (e.g., neurotic guilt)
_____e. Eleda	5. Unresolved Anger (e.g., someone has never forgiven his father for leaving the family)
_____f. Darlene	
_____g. Carlos	6. Relational Problems (e.g., marital discord)
_____h. Chuck	7. Negative Thinking (e.g., a person views everything negatively)

❖

2. As you review the case histories, match the name of the person with the category you feel best explains his or her depression.

3. As you review the causes suggested above, can you think of any other reasons why someone might experience depression?

Though there are many causes for depression, the good news is that there is hope. God is greater than any circumstance, situation, or emotion.

Focusing on God's Word

Elijah was truly a man of God and yet he experienced severe depression, to the point of wanting to die. On Mount Carmel, Elijah had challenged the prophets of Baal to a confrontation. The real God was to answer by sending fire down. Though the prophets begged their gods to send down fire, none came. Only the true God, the God of Abraham, Isaac and Jacob, was able to send down fire. It was a victory of monumental significance, and yet, despite the victory Elijah experienced severe depression.

❖❖❖❖❖❖❖❖❖❖❖❖❖❖❖❖❖❖❖❖❖❖❖❖❖

Now Ahab told Jezebel everything Elijah had done and how he had killed all the prophets with the sword. So Jezebel sent a messenger to Elijah to say, "May the gods deal with me, be it ever so severely, if by this time tomorrow I do not make your life like that of one of them."

Elijah was afraid and ran for his life. When he came to Beersheba in Judah, he left his servant there, while he himself went a day's journey into the desert. He came to a broom tree, sat down under it and prayed that he might die. "I have had enough, LORD," he said. "Take my life; I am no better than my ancestors." Then he lay down under the tree and fell asleep.

All at once an angel touched him and said, "Get up and eat." He looked around, and there by his head was a cake of bread baked over hot coals, and a jar of water. He ate and drank and then lay down again.

The angel of the LORD came back a second time and touched him and said, "Get up and eat, for the journey is too much for you." So he got up and ate and drank. Strengthened by that food, he traveled forty days and forty nights until he reached Horeb, the mountain of God. (1 Kings 19:1–8)

1. Though Elijah had just witnessed God's mighty power in sending down fire from heaven, he, nevertheless, experienced depression. Have you ever experienced depression after some major event or achievement?

2. To what might you attribute depression after a major event in your life?

3. Elijah fled to the desert. What did he experience in the desert?

Now, read 1 Kings 19:9–16.

There he [Elijah] went into a cave and spent the night.

And the word of the LORD came to him: "What are you doing here, Elijah?"

He replied, "I have been very zealous for the LORD God Almighty. The Israelites have rejected Your covenant, broken down Your altars, and put Your prophets to death with the sword. I am the only one left, and now they are trying to kill me too."

The LORD said, "Go out and stand on the mountain in the presence of the LORD, for the LORD is about to pass by."

Then a great and powerful wind tore the mountains apart and shattered the rocks before the LORD, but the LORD was not in the wind. After the wind there was an earthquake, but the LORD was not in the earthquake. After the earthquake came a fire, but the Lord was not in the fire. And after the fire came a gentle whisper. When Elijah heart it, he pulled his cloak over his face and went out and stood at the mouth of the cave.

Then a voice said to him, "What are you doing here, Elijah?"

He replied, "I have been very zealous for the LORD God Almighty. The Israelites have rejected Your covenant, broken down Your altars, and put Your prophets to death with the sword. I am the only one left, and now they are trying to kill me too."

The LORD said to him, "Go back the way you came, and go to the Desert of Damascus. When you get there, anoint Hazael king over Aram. Also, anoint Jehu son of Nimshi king over Israel, and anoint Elisha son of Shaphat from Abel Meholah to succeed you as prophet." (1 Kings 19:9–16)

21

4. Go back and underline those words and/or phrases from 1 Kings 19:9–16 that indicate Elijah's depression.

5. In what ways did the LORD encourage, comfort, and strengthen Elijah?

❖❖❖❖❖❖❖❖❖❖❖❖❖❖❖❖❖❖❖❖❖❖❖❖❖❖

Just as Elijah cowered under a tree, depressed, so did Adam and Eve after they had sinned. And just as God came to rescue Elijah, so God came to rescue Adam, Eve, and all mankind. He sent His Son, Jesus Christ, to suffer and die on the cross to rescue us and all people from sin, death, and the power of the devil.

He Himself bore our sins in His body on the tree, so that we might die to sins and live for righteousness; by His wounds you have been healed. (1 Peter 2:24)

❖❖❖❖❖❖❖❖❖❖❖❖❖❖❖❖❖❖❖❖❖❖❖❖❖❖

Focusing on My Life

1. Review the causes for depression. Circle any of them which have caused you or someone you love to experience depression. If you feel comfortable doing so, share the reasons with a partner.

2. How does knowing the cause(s) help us deal with depression?

3. It is important to know that identifying the cause for depression doesn't keep us from taking responsibility. Why might it be valuable to say there is a "statue of limitations" on what or whom you can blame for the depression you experience?

4. How did God through His Word spoken to Elijah provide Elijah comfort, encouragement, and strength to carry on? How can and will God's Word provide you comfort, encouragement, and the strength to carry on? Read the following Scripture passages for insight.

Your Word is a lamp to my feet and a light for my path. (Psalm 119:105)

As the rain and the snow come down from heaven, and do not return to it without watering the earth and making it bud and flourish, so that it yields seed for the sower and bread for the eater, so is my Word that goes out from my mouth: It will not return to me empty, but will accomplish what I desire and achieve the purpose for which I sent it. You will go out in joy and be led forth in peace; the mountains and hills will burst into song before you, and all the trees of the field will clap their hands. (Isaiah 55:10–12)

All Scripture is God-breathed and is useful for teaching, rebuking, correcting and training in righteousness, so that the man of God may be thoroughly equipped for every good work. (2 Timothy 3:16–17)

❖❖❖❖❖❖❖❖❖❖❖❖❖❖❖❖❖❖❖❖❖❖❖❖❖❖❖

5. 1 Kings 19:10–16 records a dialog between God and Elijah. God's Word came to Elijah. Elijah responded to God's Word. How is this event like worship? like a Bible study? How can worship and Bible study help you as you struggle with depression?

Focusing on the Week Ahead

Continue writing in your journal. Record some thoughts you might have about the causes for your depression. Once you've recorded your thoughts, ask God to help you move forward, out of depression and into a world of hope and promise.

❖

Closing

Read aloud Psalm 119:105; Isaiah 55:10–13; and 2 Timothy 3:16–17. Meditate on the power of God's Word. Pray that as you hear and study God's Word that the Holy Spirit would flood you with comfort, healing, and encouragement.

❖

Depression: How Can I Cope with It?

Focusing Our Sights

It's one thing to know the symptoms and the causes of depression, but quite another thing to know how to cope with it. In this session we'll consider several ways of dealing with depression, including one important method suggested by Dr. Albert Ellis known as the "ABCs" of emotional life. We'll also see that any method must be used in light of what God says in His Holy Word.

Focusing Our Attention

There are a variety of theories and philosophies about the treatment of depression.

With pen in hand underline the ways each of the following people dealt with their depression.

A. "Buzz" Aldrin was one of the first astronauts to the moon. Upon returning to earth he experienced depression. By talking with others about his feelings, he was able to overcome his depression.

B. "Ernest Hemingway's father committed suicide while struggling with severe depression.

Later in life, Ernest experienced wild mood swings, sometimes violent, which had already evoked recurrent thoughts of suicide. He had become a living replica of his father, from the list of his physical and mental ailments to peculiarities of habit and personality. Within days after his last hospital stay, which did little to relieve the dreaded bouts of depression, he came to a decision. He returned to the familiar. Again he took up the rifle and headed out into the woods in search of solace" (Stephen Arterburn, Hand-Me-Down Genes and Second-Hand Emotions, Thomas Nelson Publishers, Nashville, 1992, pp. 125–126).

C. Patty Duke had her own television show. She recorded several best-selling records. She was elected President of the Screen Actors Guild, and yet, Patty Duke struggled with severe bouts of depression. During these times she would do everything from breaking dishes to being involved sexually with men she hardly knew. However, with prescribed medication and professional counseling, Patty Duke regained control of her life.

D. Charles Spurgeon is considered one of the greatest preachers of all time. His sermons are filled with deep theological insights and with creative illustrations; nevertheless, he battled constantly with depression. Through prayer and the study of God's Word he was able to maintain some balance in his life.

How have you or someone you know dealt with depression?

❖

Focusing on the Issue

The good news is that depression can be treated. It doesn't have to follow you around like a "black dog" as it did for Winston Churchill. No matter how serious the depression may be, it can be improved through avenues that God provides. Just as God offers us physical healing through medication and skilled medical doctors, so He offers us psychological and mental help through medication and professional counselors. Sometimes the healing comes after much prayer. Sometimes it comes after a person modifies his routine or takes a much-needed vacation.

Dr. Albert Ellis, a noted therapist, gives us a helpful approach to assist us in dealing with depression, especially depression caused in part by negative or distorted thinking. He calls it the "ABCs" of emotional life.

A = those forces that have activated the situation. It might include any of the causes mentioned in session 2.

B = the beliefs—what you tell yourself—about the situation. It includes the thoughts you have about what happened. These thoughts may be irrational and terribly negative. In reality the situation may be opening up new possibilities.

C = the feelings you have because of what you tell yourself about the situation. This also includes the behavior elicited by the situation, such as, a feeling of depression or going out and getting drunk.

Experts tell us that most people think C is caused by A. However, in reality one's beliefs (B) about the activating situation (A) evokes certain feelings and behaviors (C).

❖

1. Write the "ABCs" of each of the following case studies.

Case Study 1: Denise and Dennis are engaged to be married. Two weeks before the marriage, Dennis walks out on her, and the wedding is called off. Denise goes into deep depression. She talks about being "embarrassed and ashamed over the whole situation." She believes she is now doomed to live the rest of her life alone. She is further convinced all men are louses and she never wants to date another one again.

A =

B =

C =

Case Study 2: Frank receives a derogatory review from his boss. He is told his work is sloppy and often filled with mistakes. He is so depressed over the review that for days he sits in front of his computer hardly able to function. At home he barely communicates, often going to bed immediately after dinner and sleeping until he has to go to work again the next morning. He is convinced that he is going to be fired after his next review and that he will be unable to provide for his family.

❖

A =

B =

C =

Case Study 3: Louise is a model. Though her career has been stressful, she has enjoyed it immensely. At her 25th birthday party, her agent jokingly tells her that she has "to make hay while she can," because as she gets older she will get fewer and fewer modeling jobs. After the party, her agent's words haunt her to the point where she is almost unable to function. Her energy level diminishes. She never seems to smile anymore, often appearing lethargic. She keeps asking herself, "My whole life has been modeling. What will I do when I can't do this anymore?"

A =

B =

C =

After a person identifies the "ABCs," he or she can then add two additional steps to the process known as "D" and "E."

(Siang-Yang Tan and John Ortberg, Jr., *Coping with Depression*, Baker Books, Grand Rapids, MI, 1995, pp. 78–79.)

D = the disputations or the distorted thoughts recorded under B.

E = the "eventual effects of the disputations on your feelings and behavior."

For example, in Case Study 1 the Disputation, or D, might sound like this:

"I am sincerely hurt and disappointed that Dennis called off the wedding. Though I'm ashamed it happened, it isn't the end of the world. Even though some of my family may be talking about it, they don't know the whole situation. Dennis doesn't represent every man in the world. There are lots of good men. Look at my father!"

The E or the Eventual Effect might sound like this:

"I'm still feeling bad about it, but at least I'm able to function again. In fact, I was even able to laugh over the whole situation with some of my cousins the other day. They've even lined me up with a blind date! Though I'm scared, they've convinced me I've got to start testing the waters again."

2. Write possible D's and E's for the other two case studies.

Case Study 2

D =

E =

Case Study 3
D =

E =

It is important to remember that this approach is only one of many. As we have seen in a previous session, not all depression is caused by negative thinking. Christian counselors, such as Siang-Yang Tan and John Orberg, Jr., remind us that "the task of thinking involves more than simply learning to think in ways that are less likely to lead to depression."

The follower of Christ is invited to be transformed into a new kind of person by the "renewing of the mind" (Rom. 12:2). This involves a whole new way of regarding yourself, your world, and your future. You are someone who is loved by God, accountable to God, and precious to God. At the same time, Scripture makes it clear that as sinful people we all engage in thinking from a much different vantage point (Rom. 1:21, 28). Therefore, the task of "relearning how to think" goes beyond simply becoming more "rational," or "realistic" in our thought processes. ... The goal of the follower of Christ is to learn how to think with the mind of Christ

❖

(2 Cor. 10:5), to have the same way of thinking that characterized the life of Jesus (Phil. 2:5). It is to learn to think the same way Jesus would think if He were in the body. ... Our goal therefore is not just to learn to think more "rationally" but also more Christianly.

(Siang-Yang Tan, John Ortberg, Jr., pp. 72–73.)

Remember, God transforms our thinking—minds, attitudes, feelings—by the power of the Holy Spirit working through His Word. God promises to work in and through us as we hear, read, study, and meditate on His Word.

Focusing on God's Word

Read Psalm 42. How would you describe its author, David, as he wrote it?

❖❖❖❖❖❖❖❖❖❖❖❖❖❖❖❖❖❖❖❖❖❖❖❖❖

¹As the deer pants for streams of water,
    so my soul pants for You, O God.
²My soul thirsts for God, for the living God.
    When can I go and meet with God?
³My tears have been my food
    day and night,
while men say to me all day long,
    "Where is your God?"
⁴These things I remember
    as I pour out my soul:
how I used to go with the multitude,
    leading the procession to the house of
        God,
with shouts of joy and thanksgiving
    among the festive throng.
⁵Why are you downcast, O my soul?
    Why so disturbed within me?
Put your hope in God,
    for I will yet praise Him,
    my Savior and ⁶my God.

❖

My soul is downcast within me;
        therefore I will remember You
from the land of the Jordan,
        the heights of Hermon—the Mount Mizar.
[7]Deep calls to deep
        in the roar of Your waterfalls;
all Your waves and breakers
        have swept over me.
[8]By day the LORD directs His love,
        at night His song is with me—
        a prayer to the God of my life.
[9]I say to God my Rock,
        "Why have You forgotten me?
Why must I go about mourning,
        oppressed by the enemy?"
[10]My bones suffer mortal agony
        as my foes taunt me,
saying to me all day long,
        "Where is your God?"
[11]Why are you downcast, O my soul?
        Why so disturbed within me?
Put your hope in God,
        for I will yet praise Him,
        my Savior and my God.

❖❖❖❖❖❖❖❖❖❖❖❖❖❖❖❖❖❖❖❖❖❖❖❖❖❖

1. Though the details of David's depression may be somewhat different from ours, his experience is very similar. Identify the verses that show his

a. spiritual weakness

b. self-pity

c. withdrawal

d. introspection

2. David did something more helpful than swim in self-pity, he looked to the One who could help him get out of depression—God Himself. Note the verses that tell us some of the things David did that helped him through God's guidance and counsel overcome his depression.

a. honesty about being depressed

b. honesty in talking to God about it

c. honest in why he was depressed (cf., 2 Sam. 11)

d. looking toward God for help

Because of Jesus' death and resurrection, we are reminded that no depression is too deep for God to help us through; nothing we have done, thought, or said is too great for God to forgive; nothing we can or might experience can separate us from God's love for us in Christ Jesus.

❖

3. With pen in hand underline the promise that is ours because of Jesus' resurrection.

❖❖❖❖❖❖❖❖❖❖❖❖❖❖❖❖❖❖❖❖❖❖❖❖❖❖❖❖

I pray also that the eyes of your heart may be enlightened in order that you may know the hope to which He has called you, the riches of His glorious inheritance in the saints, and His incomparably great power for us who believe. That power is like the working of His mighty strength, which He exerted in Christ when He raised Him from the dead and seated Him at His right hand in the heavenly realms. (Ephesians 1:18–20)

❖❖❖❖❖❖❖❖❖❖❖❖❖❖❖❖❖❖❖❖❖❖❖❖❖❖❖❖

Focusing on My Life

In the last few years the Associated Press has carried several stories about people who have died because they refused the medical care that was available to them. In Florida, a child dies because the family refuses to let the doctors give him a badly needed blood transfusion. The family believes that blood transfusions are forbidden by God. In Missouri, a father dies because he and his wife refuse to see a doctor after he was bitten repeatedly by a rattlesnake during a religious ceremony.

Though most people would see the foolishness in such thinking, some of these same people think it's foolish to seek professional and medical help in treating depression. Many pastors hear, "I don't want to be on medication the rest of my life!" or "Psychologists are kooky themselves or they wouldn't have become psychologists. Why should I go to them?"

1. Discuss your feelings regarding the fol-

❖

lowing avenues of help in dealing with depression:

a. Medication

b. Counseling

c. Changing one's environment

d. Prayer

e. Bible study and worship

f. Other

2. How can the words in Philippians 4:11–13 help during a time of depression?

3. How might the advice given in Philippians 3:13–14 and Ephesians 4:31–32 help when depression surfaces because of past experiences or events?

4. Write a prayer asking God to give you the wisdom needed in getting the help you need in overcoming your depression.

Focusing on the Week Ahead

Continue your daily journal. If you feel some of your depression is due to distorted thinking, try working through the suggested "ABCDEs" of your emotional life as suggested above.

Closing

Recite Psalm 42 once again. Then close by praying the prayer you wrote.

Depression: How Can I Help Others?

4

Focusing Our Sights

Though we are told to "carry each other's burdens," we are often perplexed by how to best help people who are burdened. In this session we will discuss some concrete ways to help the depressed. We will also talk about how to provide a warm and friendly climate in the local congregation for those who feel burdened.

Focusing Our Attention

Have you ever talked with someone in the hope that he or she would have some helpful word for you only to discover that you felt worse after talking with him or her? Sometimes even the comments we make to help someone can come out wrong and prove to be more harmful than helpful.

Which comments do you think might be most helpful? Which might actually be offensive?

1. Ronnie suffers from depression. In desperation she goes to her pastor. As she tells him about how she's feeling, he says:

a. "You're not really feeling that way!"

b. "You know Ronnie, if you only had more faith you wouldn't feel the way you do!"

c. "Ronnie, I get the feeling that at times you almost like being depressed!"

d. "I'll do anything you want me to, but you'll have to tell me what that is."

e. "Just pray ...!"

f. "You know, I have the name of a wonderful Christian counselor who has been extremely helpful to a number of parishioners."

2. During a break at work, a fellow employee talks to you about wanting to end his life. He tells you everything is going wrong and he can't deal with it any longer. You try to help him by saying:

a. "I think you've got a problem too big for me to handle. You'd better find someone else to talk to."

b. "What are you saying? You have so much to live for, why would you want to do something like that?"

c. "That's crazy man!"

d. "If you do, you'll go straight to hell."

e. "Do you have a plan on how you might actually take your life?"

3. Though Bernice is married, she feels terribly alone. Her husband seldom talks with her. Her one source of happiness—her children—are married and out of the home. She finds it difficult to cope with her loneliness. One night she tries to talk to her husband about her depression. Her husbands responds:

a. "Why are you laying this one on me? You're just out to punish me, aren't you?"

b. "How in the world can you expect to feel good when all day long you waste your time watching those stupid soaps and talk shows?"

c. "Don't worry, I love you."

d. "Just tell me what you want me to do about it and I'll do it."

e. "Let's talk to our pastor to see if he can help us work through some of this."

Focusing on the Issue

Motivated by the love God has demonstrate to all people through His only Son's death on the cross, His people respond by showing their love to others. St. Paul speaks of such response in Galatians 6:2, 9–10.

❖❖❖❖❖❖❖❖❖❖❖❖❖❖❖❖❖❖❖❖❖❖❖❖❖

Carry each other's burdens, and in this way you will fulfill the law of Christ. Let us not become weary in doing good, for at the proper time we will reap a harvest if we do not give up. Therefore, as we have opportunity, let us do good to all people, especially to those who belong to the family of believers. (Galatians 6:2, 9–10)

❖❖❖❖❖❖❖❖❖❖❖❖❖❖❖❖❖❖❖❖❖❖❖❖❖

1. Though you may sincerely want to help someone who is depressed, you may question whether you're qualified to do anything. What fears do you have about helping someone who's depressed?

2. During times when you've experienced depression, who helped you the most? Describe how he/she helped. Did you find help from your church? your pastor?

Stephen Arterburn in his book *Hand-Me-Down Genes and Second-Hand Emotions* reminds us that we all need a "system of support—people working together to help us in our recovery." In order to be a part of that support, he writes that we shouldn't:

- go to a psychiatrist or psychologist who dismisses our values, beliefs, and commitments.
- go to a psychiatrist or psychologist who discounts the role of God in our ultimate recovery.
- go to a therapist or counselor who believes that there is only one cause of depression and ignores all other possible contributing factors.
- go to a counselor or pastor who believes that all depression is the result of a spiritual lack of faith or disobedience on our part and can be cured without responsibly facing the medical realities known to cause depression.
- go to a counselor who condemns us as being unspiritual for accepting help from medical doctors and counselors who are experienced in dealing with depression.

- look to a counselor to help us reestablish a stable view of life if the person's therapeutic principles or worldview is opposed to our biblical position.
- confide in someone who will break our confidence for the purpose of making an "example" of us, shaming us into submission, or magnifying our past and insisting that we magically "snap out of it" and give God glory.

(Stephen Arterburn, *Hand-Me-Down Genes and Second-Hand Emotions,* Thomas Nelson Publishers, Nashville, 1992, pp. 88–89.)

3. Though we might agree with Arterburn's suggestions, why is it often difficult to find such a counselor, psychologist, or psychiatrist? Write down some questions you feel would be important to ask any counselor before you would go to or recommend him or her?

4. In an earlier session we talked about the fact that some depression is due to distorted thinking. How might we help the person who has somehow come to believe

a. that he should "never be discouraged" as it says in the hymn "What a Friend We Have in Jesus"?

b. that he is incompetent and unable to accomplish anything worthwhile?

c. that he simply cannot forget past injustices or past failures?

❖

d. that if he feels a certain way it must be an accurate picture of reality?

e. that he is getting what he deserves?

The church is a community. In a community there is interpersonal sharing and caring. A picture of such caring is given in Acts 2:42–47.

They devoted themselves to the apostles' teaching and to the fellowship, to the breaking of bread and to prayer. Everyone was filled with awe, and many wonders and miraculous signs were done by the apostles. All the believers were together and had everything in common. Selling their possessions and goods, they gave to anyone as he had need. Every day they continued to meet together in the temple courts. They broke bread in their homes and ate together with glad and sincere hearts, praising God and enjoying the favor of all the people. And the Lord added to their number daily those who were being saved. (Acts 2:42–47)

4. In what ways does your church provide care for the depressed? In what ways might your church be more intentional in helping depressed people or others who are experiencing emotional heartache?

Focusing on God's Word

In a day and age when studies tell us that depression is on the rise, the church is being called to action. As Christians "we also rejoice in God through our Lord Jesus Christ, through whom we have received reconciliation" (Romans 5:11). Through Jesus' life, death, and resurrection God reconciled us—restored the broken relationship that existed between us and Him because of sin. However, reconciliation doesn't end with God. Jesus' love for us empowers reconciliation between people. St. Paul reminds us what reconciliation between people looks like.

❖❖❖❖❖❖❖❖❖❖❖❖❖❖❖❖❖❖❖❖❖❖❖❖❖

Love is patient, love is kind. It does not envy, it does not boast, it is not proud. It is not rude, it is not self-seeking, it is not easily angered, it keeps no record of wrongs. Love does not delight in evil but rejoices with the truth. It always protects, always trusts, always hopes, always perseveres. Love never fails. (1 Corinthians 13:4–8a)

❖❖❖❖❖❖❖❖❖❖❖❖❖❖❖❖❖❖❖❖❖❖❖❖❖

1. How might you show a depressed person
a. a love that is patient?

b. a love that is kind?

c. a love that is not proud?

d. a love that is not easily angered?

e. a love that hopes?

f. a love that never fails?

2. Do you agree with the statement made by a professor of pastoral therapy to his students, "Whenever you counsel someone, see yourself in that person. If you can't, you will never really be able to empathize and help that person"? Explain your answer.

Focusing on My Life

Thomas à Kempis once said, "First keep the peace within yourself, then you can bring peace to others." You can't give to others what you yourself don't have.

1. Listed are important ingredients to good mental health. Check those items which are currently present in your life.

___ a. having a personal relationship with Jesus Christ (Matthew 22:37)

___ b. attending worship regularly

___ c. studying God's Word

❖

___ d. receiving the Lord's Supper often

___ e. thinking positively as opposed to negatively (Philippians 4:8)

___ f. effectively dealing with anger (Ephesians 4:26)

___ g. maintaining close friendships (Ecclesiastes 4:9–10)

___ h. daily working on a close, warm relationship with your family (Galatians 6:10)

___ i. reaching out to others (Matthew 22:29)

___ j. refusing to get into a routine and becoming bored

___ k. studying God's Word daily (2 Timothy 3:16–17)

___ l. not becoming too introspective

___ m. praying regularly (James 5:16)

___ n. responding rationally instead of reacting irrationally

___ o. laughing

2. As you review the list above, write 3–4 specific things you feel you need to do so that God might use you to help others.

3. Review with the other participants the most valuable things you've learned in the last four weeks. Then offer a prayer of thanks for these things.

Focusing on the Week Ahead

If you've found writing in your journal helpful, continue doing so. In the next week make up some Broad Goals as well as some Smart Goals for yourself. Broad Goals are those things that are far-reaching, big, and directive. Smart Goals are more specific and measurable and can be reached in a day or so.

Closing

Close by praying a prayer attributed to St. Francis of Assisi:

Lord, make me an instrument
 of Thy peace.
Where there is hatred, let me sow love;
where there is injury, pardon;
where there is doubt, faith;
where there is despair, hope;
where there is darkness, light;
where there is sadness, joy.
O Divine Master, grant that I may
 not so much seek to be consoled, as to
 console; to be understood, as to
 understand; to be loved, as to love.
For it is in giving that we receive;
 it is in pardoning that we are pardoned;
 it is in dying that we are born to
 eternal life.
  Amen.

Leaders Notes

Session 1

Depression: What Is It?

❖ Focusing Our Sights

(*About 2 minutes.*) Read aloud and discuss briefly the opening paragraph.

❖ Focusing Our Attention

(*About 8 minutes.*) Invite a volunteer to read aloud the opening paragraph.

1. Have participants complete the checklist independently. Then tell participants that statements A, B, F, G, and H. are true. The rest are false. Studies have shown that depression is no respecter of age. It can even occur in infancy. Scripture gives us examples of God's people struggling with depression (e.g., Jonah, Elijah, Jeremiah). Research has proven that unresolved anger is one of the reasons for depression. Some types of depression can run in families.

2. Have participants complete independently the sentence starters. Then invite volunteers to share their responses. Ask those who share their responses to validate them. Accept all reasonable responses.

❖ Focusing on the Issue

(*About 15 minutes.*) Invite volunteers to read aloud the opening paragraphs. Invite participants to discuss the two bullets.

1. Read aloud and invite volunteers to read aloud the vignettes. Urge participants to underline the symptoms of depression.

a. The symptoms JoAnne experiences are inability to work and the desire to sleep all the time.

b. Larry is unable to eat. His eating habits have changed since his father's death.

c. Elaine is unable to forgive herself and experiences guilt.

d. John and Mary's sexual activity has decreased. John has little drive.

e. Eleda is tired all the time. She has low blood sugar.

f. Darlene contemplates suicide.

g. Carlos never dealt with his anger toward his wife and brother. Carlos lives with fear. He deals with everything in a pessimistic way.

h. Chuck seems to daydream.

As you reviewed the case studies, participants may have noted the following symptoms: change in sleep patterns; change in appetite; neurotic guilt; change in a person's sex drive; excessive fatigue; thoughts and talks about suicide; seeing things out of perspective; and lack of concentration.

2. Answers will vary.

3. Answers will vary. Some possible reason may include the breakdown of the family, weakening morals, and the need for two incomes.

4. Both religious and nonreligious people sin and experience the effects of sin in this world. Even Christians are not exempt from the work of Satan in this world. But only Christians in repentance confessing their sins, have the assurance of God's forgiveness for them in Christ.

❖ Focusing on God's Word

(*About 15 minutes.*) Read aloud the opening paragraph.

1. Invite volunteers to read aloud the Scripture references. Have participants underline the symptoms of depres-

sion described in each. Job indicates that he has no peace, no quietness, and no rest. Jonah asks God to take his life. Elijah prays that he might die.

Read aloud the paragraphs that follow the Scripture references.

Jesus' struggle is evidenced in the words grief, distress of mind, depressed, and dying of sorrow.

Invite a volunteer to read aloud the paragraph following the Scripture reference to Jesus in Gethsemane. Remind participants that nothing can separate them from the love of God in Christ Jesus. The Holy Spirit working through God's Word strengthens the faith of believers.

2. Read aloud or invite a volunteer to read aloud 2 Corinthians 5:17. Invite participants to respond to the question that follows the verse. Answers will vary. Although we or someone we love may experience depression we can rely upon the faith that God has provided to us to give us new hope, new peace, and new life.

3. Answers will vary. Christ demonstrated that He had the last word over sin, death, and the power of the devil when He rose victorious from the grave. His victory is our victory. Nothing can or will separate us from Jesus' love for us.

❖ Focusing on My Life

(*About 10 minutes.*)

1. Invite volunteers to read aloud the quotations made by famous people who experienced depression. Ask, "Have you or someone you've known made similar statements?"

2. Remind participants that God provides the means through which their faith is strengthened—opportunities to experience His Word. Whenever and wherever God's Word is proclaimed, the Holy Spirit works to strengthen faith and empower us to serve God and others.

3. Urge participants to write Psalm 23 on a Post-It note or index card and place it where they will see it often.

❖ Focusing on the Week Ahead

(*About 2 minutes.*) Urge participants to complete the suggested activity prior to the next session.

❖ Closing

(*About 5 minutes.*) Complete the activities suggested in the study guide.

❖

Session 2

Depression:
What's the Reason?

❖ Focusing Our Sights

(*About 2 minutes.*) Read aloud and discuss briefly the opening paragraph.

❖ Focusing Our Attention

(*About 10 minutes.*) Invite a volunteer to read aloud the quotation from Plutarch. Discuss the questions that follow.

1. Although depression is not contagious like a cold or flu, being around someone who is depressed can cause others to become depressed or, at least, filled with anxiety.

2. Living with someone who struggles with depression can cause those who live with the depressed person to carry heavy burdens. Depression affects the entire family and all who come in close contact with a depressed person.

3. Answers will vary.

4. Negativism breeds negativism. A person who must live and/or work with a negative person can find his or her thoughts becoming negative.

❖ Focusing on the Issue

(*About 15 minutes.*) Read aloud the opening paragraph. Then invite volunteers to reread the case studies.

54

1. Urge participants to underline the probable cause of each person's depression. Emphasize that causes they may identify are mostly speculative. We cannot presume to make an accurate diagnosis with so little information. Also, professionals—counselors, psychologists, and psychiatrists—are the only ones trained to diagnose depression and its causes.

a. JoAnne's depression probably stems from her unstable life as a child.

b. The death of his father is the underlying cause of Larry's depression.

c. Elaine's guilt causes her to become depressed.

d. John's job loss has caused his depression.

e. Eleda's physical condition, low blood sugar, could be the cause of her depression.

f. Darlene's recent loss and the overwhelming burden of raising three children has caused her to become depressed.

g. Carlos' unresolved anger toward his wife and his brother have caused his depression.

h. Chuck's anticipated retirement has caused his recent depression.

2. Have participants complete the matching activity independently. Answers may vary. Then share the following probable answers: A. 2 or 5; B. 3; C. 3 or 4; D. 3 or 6; E. 1; F. 3 or 6; G. 5, 6, and/or 7; H. 3 or 7.

3. Answers will vary.

Read aloud the closing paragraph.

❖ Focusing on God's Word

(*About 20 minutes.*) Read aloud or invite a volunteer to read aloud the opening paragraph. Then have participants read aloud portions of 1 Kings 19:1–8.

1. Answers will vary.

2. Depression that follows a major event might be attributed to stress, unfulfilled expectations, exhaustion, and/or negative thinking. Answers may vary.

3. The angel of the LORD came to Elijah. The angel fed Elijah and gave him something to drink.

Invite volunteers to read aloud portions of 1 Kings 19:9–16.

4. Elijah hides in a cave and continues to repeat himself when speaking to the LORD. Remind participants that earlier Elijah asked God to take his life.

5. The *word of the LORD* came to Elijah. The LORD encouraged Elijah through His Word. Remind participants that God continues to encourage, comfort, and strengthen us today as the Holy Spirit works through His Word.

Read aloud the closing paragraph. Emphasize the forgiveness God provides to all through His Son's death on the cross. Jesus Christ rescues us in our time of need.

❖ Focusing on My Life

(*About 10 minutes.*)

1. Allow participants to share.

2. If we know the cause of depression, we can receive assistance that gets at the root of the depression.

3. Blaming others or events can keep us from acknowledging our problem and seeking help to overcome the problem. Blame cannot relieve or cure depression. If anything, blame will only cause depression to deepen.

4. God demonstrated His care and concern for Elijah as He spoke to Him. God's Word has power to transform even the most troubled soul. God continues to speak to us today through His Word, providing for us His comfort, encouragement, and the strength to carry on.

Read aloud the Scripture passages. Ask, "What insight do these passages provide to you?"

5. God continues to speak to us today through His Word. His Word is spoken in worship and Bible study. In worship God speaks to us and we respond to Him in thankfulness and praise. The Holy Spirit works through God's Word to strengthen our faith enabling us to find healing for depression.

❖ Focusing on the Week Ahead

(*About 2 minutes.*) Urge participants to complete the suggested activity prior to the next time you meet.

❖ Closing

Read aloud Psalm 119:105; Isaiah 55:10–13; and 2 Timothy 3:16–17. Allow time for brief meditation on God's Word. Then pray that the Holy Spirit would flood you with comfort, healing, and encouragement.

Session 3

Depression: How Can I Cope with It?

❖ Focusing Our Sights

(*About 2 minutes.*) Read aloud and briefly discuss the opening paragraph.

❖ Focusing Our Attention

(*About 10 minutes.*) Read aloud the opening paragraph. Then direct participants to underline the ways in which each of the famous people dealt with depression.

A. "Buzz" Aldrin talked about his feelings and was able to overcome his depression.

B. Ernest Hemingway committed suicide.

C. Patty Duke demonstrated deviant behaviors when struggling with depression. Medication and professional counseling have enabled Patty Duke to regain control of her life.

D. Charles Spurgeon prayed and studied God's Word in order to control depression that spread over his life.

❖ Focusing on the Issue

(*About 15 minutes.*) Read aloud and discuss the opening paragraphs. Emphasize that one's beliefs (B) about the activating situation (A) evokes certain feelings and behaviors (C).

58

1. Have participants work together or in pairs to determine A, B, and C for each situation.

Case Study 1: A = Dennis walks out on Denise. B = Denise is embarrassed and ashamed, doomed to live her life alone. C = Denise become deeply depressed.

Case Study 2: A = Frank receives a derogatory review at work. B = Frank tells himself that he is a failure, will be fired, and not be able to support his family. C = Frank becomes severely depressed.

Case Study 3: A = Louise's agent teases her about her age. B = She tells herself that her career is almost over. She worries about what she will do when her career ends. C = Louise becomes depressed.

Read aloud the paragraphs following the case studies. Invite a volunteer to explain D and E. Read the possible disputation and eventual effect for Case Study 1. Have volunteers suggest possible disputations and eventual effects for Case Study 2 and 3.

2. Case Study 2: D = Frank tells himself that he is a good worker, who needs to work at making fewer mistakes. E = Frank makes fewer mistakes and his next performance review is better.

Case Study 3: D = Louise reminds herself that she has many years left as a model and many other gifts. E = Louise begins facing each day with enthusiasm as she continues to look forward to her future.

Read aloud the paragraphs that follow. Remind participants that God transforms our thinking by the power of the Holy Spirit working through God's Word.

❖ Focusing on God's Word

(*About 15 minutes.*) Read aloud or invite volunteers to read aloud Psalm 42. David is obviously experiencing anxiety and/or depression as he writes the psalm.

1. Have participants identify verses that show David's

spiritual weakness, self-pity, withdrawal, and introspection. Possible responses are as follows:

a. spiritual weakness — vv. 1, 2, 6.

b. self-pity — vv. 3, 4, 7, 10.

c. withdrawal — vv. 2, 9.

d. introspection — vv. 2, 5, 6, 11.

2. David was honest about his depression (vv. 1, 2, 5, 6), honest in talking with God about it (vv. 1, 5, 6, 7, 9), honest in why he is depressed (vv. 3, 10), and looking toward God for help (vv. 1, 2, 5, 6, 8, 9, 11).

Read aloud the paragraph that follows.

3. Although answers will vary, participants will probably underline enlightened, hope, power, and mighty strength.

❖ Focusing on My Life

(*About 10 minutes.*) Read aloud or invite volunteers to read aloud the opening paragraphs. Ask, "Why do people who wouldn't think twice about going to a doctor for a cold, flu, or sinus infection, resist seeking medical attention for depression?" An unfair and unwarranted stigma is often attached to seeking help from a mental health professional. This is unfortunate since mental health professionals help thousands of people who suffer from depression every year.

1. Answers will vary.

2. Philippians 4:11–13 reminds us that through Christ all things are possible, including healing from depression.

3. Philippians 3:13–14 reminds us to forget that which is behind us and press on toward the goal, the prize that is ahead of us—eternal life in heaven with Jesus. In Ephesians 4:31–32 St. Paul reminds us to forgive those who have hurt us, just as Christ has forgiven us. Forgiving and forgetting can focus our attention on healing for the future, rather than focusing our attention on that which we can do nothing—our past.

4. Invite participants to write a prayer asking God to give them wisdom in getting the help they need in overcoming depression. Save the prayers to use during the closing activity.

❖

❖ Focusing on the Week Ahead

(*About 2 minutes.*) Invite participants to complete the suggested activity prior to the next session.

❖ Closing

(*About 5 minutes.*) Read aloud Psalm 42. Then invite volunteers to share the prayers they wrote earlier.

Session 4

Depression: How Can I Help Others?

❖ Focusing Our Sights

(*About 2 minutes.*) Read aloud and discuss briefly the opening paragraph.

❖ Focusing Our Attention

(*About 10 minutes.*) Read aloud or invite a volunteer to read aloud the opening paragraphs. Read aloud the short vignettes. Then have participants choose the most helpful responses.

1. D and F are the best possible responses. Telling someone not to feel a certain way or telling them how to feel is not helpful.

2. A and B are the best possible responses. Asking probing questions and judging the individual would not be helpful.

3. C, D, and E are possible responses. This husband and wife will probably need the counsel of their pastor in order to work through the years of trouble that is infecting their relationship.

❖ Focusing on the Issue

(*About 15 minutes.*) Read aloud the opening paragraph. Then invite a volunteer to read Galatians 6:2, 9–10.

1. Answers will vary. Invite participants to share openly.

2. Again, answers will vary. Don't force anyone to share. Instead, invite volunteers to share.

Read aloud what Stephen Arterburn says we shouldn't do in order to support a person struggling with depression. Discuss the list.

3. Answers will vary. Some questions you might want to ask a counselor before going to or recommending him or her are as follows:

- Are you a confessing Christian?
- How do you treat depression?
- What do you believe is the cause of depression?

4. Again, answers will vary.

a. Christians can become discouraged. God never promised that we would never be discouraged.

b. Demonstrate to the person that they are competent and able to accomplish worthwhile things.

c. Remind this person of God's forgiveness for him in Christ Jesus. While we were still His enemies, God sent His only Son into this world to suffer and die for us.

d. Help this person to recognize that there are often many ways to look at an issue.

e. Getting even or holding a grudge will not help us deal with depression. If anything, harboring anger will only cause us to miss getting the help we need.

Read aloud Acts 2:42–47. Discuss the question that follows.

4. Answers will vary. Do not let this discussion become a gripe session. Instead focus participants' energy on how they might better help those who are depressed or experiencing emotional heartache.

❖ Focusing on God's Word

(*About 10 minutes.*) Invite a volunteer to read aloud the opening paragraph. Then invite another volunteer to read aloud 1 Corinthians 13:4–8a.

1. Answers will vary.

2. Answers will vary. Although we do need to empathize with those whom we help, we can't take on their problems. We can become too emotionally involved in a situation so that we are unable to help.

❖ Focusing on My Life

(*About 15 minutes.*) Read aloud the opening paragraph.

1. Have students check those items currently present in their lives. Then ask, "Which of the items not currently present would you like to make a part of your life?" Invite participants to share how the various items have been helpful to them.

2. Answers will vary. Invite volunteers to share their responses.

3. Share the most important things learned during the past four weeks. Then invite volunteers to offer prayers of thanks for these things.

❖ Focusing on the Week Ahead

(*About 2 minutes.*) Urge participants to complete the suggested activity.

❖ Closing

(*About 2 minutes.*) Pray together a prayer attributed to St. Francis of Assisi.